# AROUND
# BRIGHTON
# & HOVE

# AROUND
# BRIGHTON
# & HOVE

## FROM THE JUDGES POSTCARD ARCHIVE COLLECTION

## DAVE RANDLE

SUTTON PUBLISHING

Sutton Publishing Limited
Phoenix Mill · Thrupp · Stroud
Gloucestershire · GL5 2BU

First published 2007

Copyright © Dave Randle, 2007

*Title page photograph:* Night-time view of
Brighton.

**British Library Cataloguing in Publication Data**
A catalogue record for this book is available from the
British Library.

ISBN 978-0-7509-4000-9

Typeset in 10.5/13.5 Photina.
Typesetting and origination by
Sutton Publishing Limited.
Printed and bound in England.

# Acknowledgements

Many thanks to Trevor Wolford of Judges for his support and enthusiasm;
archivist John Eastlake, for making my job a great deal easier; Simon
Fletcher of Sutton Publishing for his patience and understanding; and my
long-suffering wife, Sue, for all the cataloguing, copying and other
invaluable assistance in compiling this book.

# CONTENTS

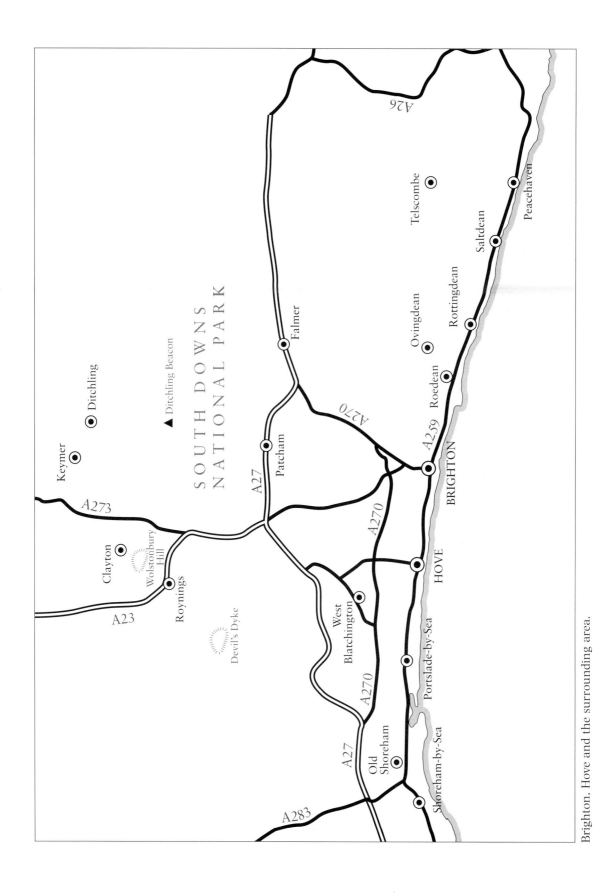

Brighton, Hove and the surrounding area.

# INTRODUCTION

Nowhere on earth has reinvented itself more times than Brighton, and few places that have been around nearly as long still retain anything like its forward-looking attitude. Most towns with a past half as glorious would be content to trade on their memories – any reinvention confined to the creation of a theme park of their former selves. Brighton's past glories stretch back into antiquity and, with equal moments of ingloriousness, have maintained an alternating current of energy that has sustained invaders, investors and inventors, artists, authors and activists throughout history. All this apart from making an honest living through fishing, agriculture and even manufacturing.

Little wonder then, perhaps, that the place seems to have as many histories as it has had incarnations. The prevailing learned opinion is that it owes its name – and its very existence – to a Saxon by the name of Beorthelm. Beorthelm's 'tun', then a sort of tribal farmstead, became 'Brighthelmstone' and some suggest it remained so until the wags of the Regency period, given as they were to pronouncing 'Featherstonehaugh' Fanshaw, pronounced it Brighton from that time on. In reality it seems to have rejoiced in a number of variations on both names for centuries although the official decision to stick with the 'Brighton' name and spelling was taken as late as the beginning of the nineteenth century.

Another claimant to the title of progenitor of the Saxon village was a bishop by the name of Brighthelm, but interestingly, and with no offence intended to Beorthelm or the good bishop, for a number of those centuries something not dissimilar to Dungeness's Helmstone existed at the place now known as the Old Steyne. As this hardened ancient riverbed was also the only safe access from the sea amid marshes and quicksands, its sarsen stone circle was likely to have been a major point of identification. Brighthelmstone, or the Brighton Helmstone? Fanciful, probably. In any case, the stones were removed before the building of St Nicholas's Church, but their memory lives on in the name of the Old Steine, which would also go on to be the cradle of fashionable Brighton.

Some accounts have the place suddenly taking up fishing in the Middle Ages, but there were certainly fishermen there when Beorthelm's longships turned up in the fifth century and logic suggests they had been harvesting such a ready source of sustenance and income from the time of the first settlers. Why else would they have placed themselves in the direct path of bloodthirsty invaders? Shortly after the Norman Conquest, the Domesday Book's researchers record the existence of a substantial fishing fleet in what was then known as Bristelemstune.

What most histories do agree on is that in 1313 the village became a town with its own council and a charter to hold various markets, including the fish market on the beach, which continued to take place until the 1960s and has recently been revived.

Over the next couple of hundred years the town expanded, turning what had once been field strips, or 'laines', into commercial streets, warehouses and dwellings of beam and thatch, while the fishing community continued to inhabit its own separate cottages and hovels at the sea's edge. Fields known as the Hempshares were set aside to grow the raw material for their nets.

Something else that is not disputed is the irritant part played by the French in much of Brighton's history. Official expeditions and privateers of one kind and another regularly put out from the neighbouring coast to further put out the town's residents. Almost exactly two hundred years after the town's formation (1513 or 1514), having swarmed ashore and liberated anything of value not nailed down, they burned the whole place to the ground.

Thirty years later they tried it again, but by then the canny inhabitants had set up a system of beacons by which to alert and mobilise the population. This time the French were driven back to their boats, suffering a number of casualties in the process. It didn't stop them, but it slowed them down for a while and gave them something to think about.

In the sixteenth and seventeenth centuries Britain was embroiled more often than not in wars with its continental neighbours and, even if they were not part of a concerted plan for invasion or conquest, expeditions to harry each other's ports and harbours went on almost incessantly. The representatives of France arriving off Brighton now were not daring corsairs but professional fighters with fully equipped naval vessels. Instead of taking their chances ashore, they opened fire with heavy cannon designed to blast the inhabitants into submission. But by this time 'Brighthamstead' had fortified itself and armed its citizens to the point where they could see off a whole fleet.

But it is the Regency period that forms most people's image of the glory of Brighton. Its translation of the town in the mid-eighteenth century to a haunt of princes and polite society could not have been more welcome proof of the old adage about it being darkest before the dawn. When traveller and author Daniel Defoe passed this way in the course of his *Tour Through the Whole Island of Great Britain*, he found a place ravaged by violent storms and economic decline, its fishing fleet decimated and its spirits low. In fact, the creator of Robinson Crusoe and Moll Flanders could not pass on quickly enough. 'Brighthelmston is a poor fishing town, old built, and on the edge of the sea', he recorded grudgingly before hastening on in the direction of Shoreham. Few would blame him. Accommodations in the town were run down and disease ridden. Because of its shingle base and its position at the bottom of the Downs and the edge of the sea, drainage was problematical to say the least. Not only could the town not cope with its own waste, it inherited that of settlements to its landward side, so open cesspools were everywhere and the public water supply was frequently contaminated.

All this changed in 1750 when a medical man from nearby Lewes wrote a book advocating the healing properties of seawater. Dr Richard Russell's catchily titled *Glandular Diseases, or a Dissertation on the Use of Sea Water in the Affections of the Glands* took a little while to catch on, but soon became a monster hit with the glanded gentry, who descended on Brighton in their droves. Affected by the assertions contained in the good doctor's dissertation, many came not merely to paddle or bathe in it, but also to drink copious quantities of the stuff. As is so often the case, Russell eventually came to believe his own publicity, moved to Brighton himself in 1759 and promptly died. He had lived to be over seventy, which was not commonplace in those days, so he might have been on to something, though imbibing the waters of the English Channel is not now seen as a keystone of primary healthcare.

Within thirty years of the book's publication the population of the town had doubled. What is now known as the demographic had also undergone a major change. The natives, who had survived those many centuries wresting a living from the sea and their meagre laines, were suddenly swamped by an inland sea of toffs and even royals. Railings were put up around the Old Steine to stop them drying their vulgar nets where the new money wanted to disport itself and, slowly but surely, service and entertainment took the place of traditional toil.

It was at this period that the Lanes began the transformation from a ramshackle rookery of fishermen's dwellings into the treasure trail of antique shops and eateries with which their name is nowadays synonymous.

By this time also, the bulky figure of the then Prince of Wales had become a regular feature of the landscape and, as the eighteenth century gave way to the nineteenth, he and his architects would complete the work of turning Brighton into the resort that would later gain the title London-by-Sea. The bijou marine pavilion that had been raised a few years earlier to accommodate Prinnie and his retinue on seaside jaunts was in need of a makeover by 1815. Never one to do things by halves, he commissioned the great John Nash to turn it into the trippy vision of an Indian temple that is now such a landmark – and such a symbol – of the place.

Entertainments and spectacles for the visitors multiplied. The piers arrived, the aquarium, the parks and gardens. Fashionable terraces, and even whole towns, would spring up over the next century as gradually the tide of titled types receded, died out or took itself orf to the continent to be replaced by less privileged citizens with new-found means.

They came by train, by charabanc, by motorcar and by motorbikes and scooters, each of them finding plenty of things – or in the case of the Mods and Rockers, people – to do in this sparkling resort on the southern edge of the newly democratised society.

And still Brighton's welcome was larger than that. Between the upper crusts and the bucket and spade brigade has always existed a less defined echelon of artists, creative types and free-thinkers, drawn by its *joie de vivre*, its possibilities, its beauty and its essentially cosmopolitan nature. And this undercurrent, more than anything else, is probably responsible for the old place's latest reinvention.

A view of Hove, late 1940s.

A melting pot of cultures, creeds, philosophies and intellects, Brighton and Hove achieved city status on 1 January 2000.

A new city for a new millennium, the new, and constantly evolving, Brighton has a long history to learn from, and a succession of past Brightons to which it owes a debt of gratitude.

This selection of postcards from the Judges archive brings various eras of Brighton, Hove and the surrounding area back to life and shows how closely that past is woven into the landscape of today.

# 1

# Brighton & Hove

One of the last piers to be built in England, R. St George Moore's Palace Pier was intended to take over from Brighton's venerable Chain Pier, which was showing major signs of decay and would be demolished once its replacement was up and running. Work on the new pier began in 1891, but financial problems dogged its builders until, in December 1896, the old pier collapsed of its own accord in a mighty storm. As if it took it all personally, its wreckage bombarded the new structure, causing a deal of damage.

The new pier was completed in 1901, by which time its cost had risen to £137,000 – an enormous amount of money in those days. This night shot shows what a spectacular addition to the town it was. Over 1,700ft long and widely regarded as the most perfect example of an English seaside pier, it still attracts over 2 million visitors a year more than a hundred years after its completion.

While merrymakers and promenaders thronged the pier and its sideshows, its elegant outline only added to the beauty of the scene. It would be many years before the slow pace of life of the town's residents gave way to the rush of pleasure-seeking incomers. In this tranquil scene from the early 1900s the *Skylark* and two other boats from Shoreham rest on the beach while a fisherman repairs his nets.

In this picture the whole fleet is inshore, and the mooring posts that once lined the beach are clearly visible.

And here, a small sailing boat allows the wind to bring it right on to the shore. These were the days when sails still ruled. A larger craft is seen passing up the Channel past the Palace Pier.

Here's a more populated shot from the early twentieth century. Apparently not much for swimming or letting it all hang out, it's not immediately obvious what the attractions of beach life were to our Edwardian ancestors. Even the fun fairs we now associate with the end of the pier would not have been present when the Palace Pier was originally opened. They were introduced as a ploy to revive waning popularity. A wonder of the age, piers had a very short heyday, lasting barely a decade.

The West Pier at Brighton is the only seaside pier to be Grade I listed. Designed by the great Eugenius Birch, its construction was begun in 1864, but immediately held up as a result of an unpredicted rise in the cost of steel. The navvies drafted in to build the epic structure were fast becoming specialists. They had just finished working on the pier at Deal before moving here to work for the contractor Laidlaw. Throughout the protracted process they lived in shacks in the undercliff.

From the time the first piles were driven in March 1864 to its completion in October 1866, the cost of the West Pier had risen by a staggering – for the time – £21,000. Laidlaw was caught between paying inflated steel prices and delaying construction in the hope that they would normalise. Both cost the firm dearly and in the end it made a loss on the project.

The Pavilion was added to the West Pier in 1893, and this picture shows the newly completed Concert Hall in 1916. The interwar period saw some revival in the pier's popularity. In busy times the footfalls of visitors would cause it to oscillate in the manner of the Millennium footbridge over the Thames in London.

The West Pier's apparently timeless splendour in photographs such as this makes its present fate seem all the more tragic. Trademark of Brighton and star of the movie version of *Oh! What A Lovely War*, the old lady has fallen on hard times. Despite major fund-raising initiatives by Spike Milligan in the 1960s and more recently Chris Eubank – and even though lottery money is earmarked for its restoration – it stands forlorn these days, a victim of wind, weather and, most of all, neglect; a stately home for starlings.

A picture dating from 1916 shows how successfully the seafront facilities at Brighton were integrated. The grand plan not only produced a thing of beauty, but also provided everything the visitor – or the local – could need for recreation. The paddling pool offered safe bathing for the tinies while their parents looked on from deck chairs.

The illuminations were another major novelty in a world where many houses still relied on oil and gas lamps. At night the whole front became an enchanted world of coloured light bulbs. Here taxis line up at the West Pier to ferry concertgoers to hotels and trains.

Structures of the scale of Palace Pier have an impact way beyond the seafront to which they are attached. The model development of Kemptown, to the east of Brighton, benefits by viewing its sunsets through the pier's exquisite silhouette. Kemptown's founder, Thomas Read Kemp (1782–1840), built himself a house here based on the Temple of Solomon. This architectural jewel, once a unique sight, is now lost among the high walls and extensions of the Brighton and Hove High School for Girls.

Two industries coexist happily in this shot from the 1930s. A fishing boat from Shoreham rests on the shingle within sight of the luxury hotels spearheading the tourism revolution. Since this was taken the fortunes of Brighton and its two flagship hotels, the Grand and the Metropole, have ebbed and flowed, whereas Shoreham today is the biggest fishing port between Brixham and Lowestoft.

*Opposite, top:* At the end of the sixteenth century Brighton had the largest fishing fleet on the south coast, with over eighty boats and four hundred men employing upward of ten thousand nets. But just a generation later, in 1665, it was practically wiped out when the sea destroyed the Lower Town.

*Opposite, bottom:* None the less, Brighton and fishing have always been synonymous, and an open fish market was held on the beach from time immemorial until 1960, when the Department of Interference stepped in. Happily, forty years on, the tradition has been revived in the area outside the Fishing Museum.

Capstan horses were immensely strong and agile. Their main employment involved turning the capstans to drag boats on to the beach – their job description including an ability to avoid tripping over the line – but they also moonlighted as furniture movers and carthorses while the fleet was at sea.

Romantically entitled 'The Glittering Sea', this image evokes a time when there was a natural, organic arrangement between man and the elements; an era before quotas, taxes and centralisation regulated the life out of it. In those far-off days the doughty fishermen of Brighton plied their watery trade as far afield as Scarborough.

The architects and planners of the new Brighton that grew from the original fishing village had their eye on the bigger picture. Little or nothing was done in isolation; buildings, gardens, walkways and piers were created on a grand plan that underpins the character of the place to this day. Like the best landscape gardeners, they created vistas and experiences for the visitor such as this one, combining the natural shoreline, the tools of the fishing industry and the offshore engineering masterpiece.

Here's another artistic framing of the front in celebration of its cohesive success. Opposite the lamp are a handcart and wheelbarrow belonging to the gardeners who maintained and adorned its architectural purity.

Not far into the twentieth century the beach is beginning to take on a more democratic quality. Beach huts and deck chairs have replaced the bathing machines of the Victorians and the scene is set for what would become the traditional British seaside holiday. Nowhere would play a larger part in its development than Brighton.

For the moment, though, more serious matters took priority on the town's beaches. While holidaymakers – and dogs – could lie down and take it easy, the fishermen had nets and boats to maintain, and the next expedition to plan.

It was rare for there to be no action on the beach, despite the low numbers of tourists; and there was no attempt to segregate the public from the activities of the fishermen. No health and safety 'issues' and no fear of vandalism, it would seem.

*Opposite, top:* Firmly planted on the shingle on a calm day was the best time to check that sails and rigging were in tip-top condition. In those days the men's lives depended on taking their own responsibility for the condition of their craft and equipment.

*Opposite, bottom:* Here's the *Skylark* in full sail, looking much more impressive than in the earlier picture (p. 12), but still seeming a fragile vessel in which to take on the might of English coastal waters.

There seemed, indeed, to be a natural harmony and sense of give and take between this traditional, timeless pursuit and the enjoyment of onlookers, especially when, as here, the workers far outnumbered them.

*Opposite, top:* But all that was about to change. The message reached Londoners that all this was only a train ride away and suddenly the boom was on. Where Edwardians had lately contemplated the empty sands to the sound of flapping sails and seabirds, all was uproar and babble and you had to get up early to get a few square yards of shingle to yourself.

*Opposite, bottom:* By the time of this picture there were even concessions to a sort of beachwear. Children could sport sun-suits, women tennis skirts and the men pioneered the poor man's answer to the newly invented military issue Bermuda shorts, the rolled-up trouser leg.

Little by little, the precedence changed and the beach became more and more the domain of the holidaymaker rather than the working fisherman. By the 1920s Victorian values were just so last century. At last you could take a day off from the daily grind. Sun-worshipping and disporting yourself in public became acceptable pastimes. The wind of change was blowing over Brighton beach, and substantial groynes helped protect the older folk from the draught.

One thing that did carry over from the earlier centuries, as noted above, was a sense of the whole. The new Brighton that emerged in response to the needs of visitors was laid out and developed to an overall plan. Superintendent of Parks in the 1920s B.K. McClaren created the town's stunning sunken gardens, since emulated by seaside towns everywhere; he was also responsible for the boating pool and the rockery opposite Preston Park.

McClaren's concepts were masterpieces of stage and people management and landscaping. Promenaders could wander through his walkways, take their ease on strategically placed benches, marvel at the council's spectacular floral displays, or go boating without straying far from the Prom.

The commercialisation and exploitation of coastal resorts was still a new science at the time. Today's residents and visitors owe a lot to the vision of Mr McClaren and his colleagues, which still ensures there is so much breathing space between the roaring road and the beach.

The fishing village had changed out of all recognition. Its wild beauty had been tamed, but was beauty none the less. An evening stroll on clean, safe, smooth landscaped paths to watch the sun set on the shimmering sea was a whole new experience.

To a generation bombarded with colourful images as we are today, these black and white photographs don't begin to convey the impact of McClaren's municipal gardens. There was such uniformity of dress, so little colour even in shop signs and advertising that these floral arrangements would have acted like an explosion to the senses.

Decorously posed on the wall, these two figures with their backs to the gardens are more interested in the passing parade on the prom, or perhaps each other.

We have to use our imagination to flood in the colour and perfume of these displays, when not mixed, as they are today, with the smell and the roar of traffic.

In this picture from the early 1960s a water feature added still further to the harmonious nature of McClaren's design, the tinkling fountains actively instilling a sense of peace.

*Opposite, top:* A safe paddling pool for children with somewhere for the parents to keep an eye on them was another fine feature of the redeveloped seafront.

*Opposite, bottom:* Originally opened in the mid-1920s, the paddling pool has become a much-loved landmark of Brighton. Recently renovated at the time of writing, it is nowadays a popular venue for musical and other events.

The boating pool in the late 1920s with the West Pier and the Metropole Hotel in the background.

As this view from the opposite angle demonstrates, the boating pool was such a popular attraction in the early days that there was barely room to move.

The almost circular boats were entirely surrounded by a buffer that protected them against almost inevitable collisions.

For eighty years the boating pool has been a still point around which much of the world has changed. This picture shows it before the Second World War . . .

. . . and this one is well into the 1950s. That's a very long time for an attraction to remain more or less unchanged, and an indicator that we're not really all that different from our ancestors.

When the time came in the 1830s to build the outer wall that would support the promenade, Brighton's coffers were far from swollen, the affluence that would come from the seaside boom still some years off. Instead of hiring professional 'navvies', therefore, William Lambert employed the town's paupers at a rate of 10s per square foot. The project was completed in three years. This picture is from the 1960s.

This view from East Cliff is slightly earlier, and shows the open-top buses lining up for business in the height of summer.

Even in the 1960s only the costumes, the Coca-Cola sign and the presence of the Mini van really denote much change from the days when the pier was built. The mixture of boats and holidaymakers continues much as before.

*Opposite, top:* Like the West Pier, Brighton Aquarium was designed by Eugenius Birch. Because the planners insisted the building must rise no higher than it neighbours on the seafront, much of the design involved underground excavation. Work began on its construction in 1869. The ambitious project, which included, in addition to its main attraction, a reading room, a conservatory and a roof terrace roller-skating rink, cost £130,000 by the time it opened in 1872. This photograph shows off the modified frontage added by the council in 1927. The original entrance featured bronze statues representing the four seasons, which have since been lost.

*Opposite, bottom:* When its then management got into financial difficulties in 1901 the aquarium was acquired by the council. By the time this photo was taken in the 1980s, it had changed management again and become a Sea-Life Centre. In recent years the aquarium, which boasts one of the longest underwater tunnels in England, became home to a number of endangered sea turtles made homeless by the closing of another collection.

Meeting House Lane gets its name from the old Presbyterian Meeting House that once stood upon it. The Lanes take their name from an Anglo-Saxon word for lease, which originally referred to the lease-held fields upon which this now fashionable area was built – initially to provide cottages for fishermen. The North Laine had no connection with the original Lanes and only acquired that name officially in 1977.

By the 1930s the character of the Lanes was already changing and, as today, you could find all sorts of curios and somewhere to go for a cup of coffee.

The box spilling flowers on to the canopy serves to highlight the increasing gentility of
Meeting House and the other Lanes as time progressed. Today, of course, they are one of the
trendiest and most visited parts of the city.

After the war change was rapid. R.J. Eales, Julian Chalcroft *et al.* swelled the numbers of antique dealers, jewellers, watchmakers and porcelain sellers setting up shop in the Lanes.

The hanging basket has made its entrance by the time of this picture of Meeting House Lane's temptingly described 'old established dining rooms'.

Looking very peaceful in this early picture, Castle Square went on to become very much a focal point for the town, and the new city. It was the natural terminus for the first omnibuses serving the town, and is now a mecca for diners and shoppers.

*Below:* Judges Postcards founder Fred Judge was one of the early exponents of night photography, an endeavour that, in the pre-exposure meter days of slow film emulsions, was very much more of an art than a science. Widespread electric illumination arrived soon afterward, turning Brighton seafront into a fairyland of white and coloured lights. This atmospheric image captures an earlier, more restrained, lighting scheme.

Far from revelling in sun and fun, these Edwardian visitors look as if they're prepared for the worst. You would think it was Vladivostok rather than King's Road.

A more romantic sunset view of the seafront in the early 1920s, with families enjoying a stroll in the gathering dusk.

As the twentieth century moved into its third decade, so the motor vehicle began to make its presence felt, as here at East Cliff. As peaceful as this appears from today's viewpoint, the inexorable change of a pace of life that had remained much the same for centuries – a change initially triggered a century earlier by the coming of the railways – was already gathering momentum.

Here's King's Road in the early 1930s, dominated as it had been since 1864 by J.H. Whichcord's Grand Hotel. The hotel was built on the site of the old Battery House, where the lieutenant in charge of Brighton's defences had been stationed until its demolition in 1858.

The Grand Hotel by night, also in the 1930s. Despite its tragic associations with the bomb attack on Margaret Thatcher's cabinet in October 1984, the Grand, now part of the prestigious De Vere chain, continues to fulfil the vision of its designer 150 years on. Only last-minute intervention with a listing order prevented its demolition in the 1960s to make way for an amusement arcade.

'Read all about it!' A newspaper seller seems not to be finding many takers among the promenaders on King's Road. Not many in the deckchairs lined up outside the Metropole either. Overlooking the West Pier, Alfred Waterhouse's magnificent hotel opened in 1890. Among the architect's many other works were the town halls at Manchester and Hove, and Strangeways prison.

*Opposite, top:* A Customs House, parade ground and a number of dwellings were cleared to make way for the Metropole, which cost £57,000 to build – a tidy sum in the 1890s, when you bear in mind you could get a room there for 3*s* 6*d*, and a full suite for £3 8*s*. There were elaborate gardens and the hotel was faced in distinctive red terracotta tiles, which contrasted with neighbouring buildings, as can be seen in this picture from the 1920s.

*Opposite, bottom:* A few more people have turned up for this shot, entitled 'By the West Pier', demonstrating again the cohesion of Brighton's public areas. The Metropole and the pier preside over an area for strolling, lounging and socialising. The motor car has cut a swathe through the middle of it these days, and there's not much left of the pier, but you can still get the idea.

Toffs could take their Rollers right down to the beach in the 1930s. When the Metropole first opened, motorists were still expected to follow a man with a red flag. To celebrate the raising of the speed limit from 4 to 14mph six years later, the first London to Brighton 'Emancipation' Run was held, with the Metropole as its finishing point.

Designed by modernist pioneer Wells Coates, Embassy Court was the 'latest thing' when it was completed in 1935, and caused more than a slight stir at the time. Resolutely modern then, it is now listed as a building of special architectural interest, but has not worn well.

In its time the distinctive high-rise has been home to numerous famous actors and artists. For years bits kept dropping off it, but its residents were and remain unanimous in their praise for the genius of its design. They formed themselves into a group called Bluestone to raise money to renovate the building and enlisted Terence Conran to oversee the restorations, which were completed in October 2005.

The general consensus is that the Old Steine derives its name from a sarsen stone circle that stood on the site of St Nicholas's church, and upon which the fishermen were wont to dry their nets. The remains of some of the stones purportedly form part of the base of the fountain seen here in Steine Gardens. It is also thought that one of the stones existed in Air Street until the 1960s, but this has since disappeared.

When the medieval parish church of St Nicholas became too small for the congregation of the rapidly expanding town, the new church of St Peter was commissioned. A competition to choose its design was won by an up-and-coming architect by the name of Charles Barry, later to gain fame and a knighthood for designing the Houses of Parliament. His original design incorporated a spire, which was never added. The foundation was laid in 1824 and the building was consecrated in 1828, although it didn't officially take on the mantle of Brighton's parish church until 1873. In the idyllic photograph opposite, the church was already a hundred years old. Above, the building had reached 150 years of age and the world had moved on around it. The church was still an oasis of calm, but its parishioners had a bit more to cope with to gain the sanctuary of its interior. The two 'no entry' signs could not, however, be blamed for falling congregations.

Originally known as the North Steine, the area that is now Victoria Gardens was the town's recreation area; but by the early 1800s it had become a 'place of shame and reproach'. The Prince Regent inaugurated a fund for its improvement with a grant of £500. The result was first known as the North Steine Enclosure. Completed in 1818, it was opened by its benefactors and owners to the public in 1883. In 1896 it was combined with the existing Southern Enclosure to form the present gardens. This view is from the 1920s.

Brighton's first and largest planned park, Preston Park, was bought from William Bennett-Stanford, then owner of Preston Park House, in 1883, for £50,000 – again, a lot of money at that time, but helped by a win on the gee-gees, or rather by a bequest of £70,000 by local bookmaker William Davies.

The park opened to the public in 1884, and offered leafy walks, landscaped vistas and brilliantly designed water elements such as this, which provided much solace to those returning from the First World War.

The defining feature of Preston Park must be the Rotunda Café. This had started life as an exhibit at the Wembley Exhibition of 1924. Brighton Council bought it and erected it at the park in 1929, where it has remained to this day, with the aid of recent restoration.

Preston Park, which the then mayor hoped 'would long be a means of enjoyment, recreation and increased health to the inhabitants', covered an area of 66 acres. It later benefited from the addition of grass tennis courts, a cricket ground, bowling greens and cycle tracks.

Queen's Park opened in 1892. Although it offers all sorts of leisure facilities, as this little chap has discovered, its lake is the main attraction. It was originally known simply as 'Brighton Park' but was renamed in honour of Queen Adelaide. Restoration, including the plugging of various leaks in the lake, was recently completed.

One of the finest springs in Europe, or so it was described, St Anne's Well is a chalybeate, or iron-bearing spring, and is also at the root of a ley line that crosses the downs. Brighton council bought the gardens in which the well is situated in 1908, for the sum of £10,000. The park is home to a unique collection of native and exotic trees.

The War Memorial in the Old Steine – one of a number in Brighton – records the names of 2,597 men and 3 women who died in the First World War. This picture commemorated its unveiling in 1922.

Even on a dull day there is something uplifting and exotic about the surreal juxtaposition of minarets and domes with all the surrounding Englishness. A marine pavilion stood on this site for some time before the prince engaged his friend and architect John Nash to turn it into a palace. Frederick Crace and Robert Jones were enlisted to create an interior to match, and the building, begun in 1815, was completed by 1818.

*Opposite:* The author of *Vanity Fair*, William Makepeace Thackeray, wrote: 'It is the fashion to run down George IV, but what myriads of Londoners ought to thank him for inventing Brighton?' There are few inventions in Europe that compare to George's Royal Pavilion – a mad pastiche of Indian and Chinese vernaculars realised by and for someone who had never seen either. Looking somewhat less incongruous in horse-drawn times, here is the stunning North Gate.

A mere thirty years later George was gone and Victoria had no interest in the place. Everything of any value had been stripped out of it and it was starting to fall into serious disrepair. Wisely, the Brighton Town Commissioners decided to buy it in 1850, making it pay for itself by hosting exhibitions and shows

in its usable salons. By this means, and as a somewhat crumbling curiosity, it continued to eke out an existence right up to the time of this photograph – just after the First World War – and beyond, as evidenced by the wheelie 'annual album' of events.

By the end of the Second World War the old place was in such a state that some people were all for pulling it down. Mercifully the voice of reason was heard and the building was shored up long enough to be fully restored in 1982, at a cost in excess of £9m.

Considering its structural woes, the Pavilion looks very sound and neatly turned out in this 1950s picture. The war was over and rationing had come to an end, and Brighton's next big popularity boom was getting under way. This must be the calm before the storm.

During the First World War
the Pavilion was used as a
hospital for Indian
servicemen. It must have
seemed like a rather
Disneyesque home from
home. The great kitchen
with its high ceiling
supported by four pillars in
the form of palm trees
served as an operating
theatre.

According to Nazi
propagandist Lord Haw-
Haw, Hitler gave special
instructions that the
Pavilion was not to be
bombed by the Luftwaffe.
If his invasion plan had
succeeded, he intended to
use it as his headquarters.

You could park next to the
Pavilion in the early 1960s,
and nobody minded which
way you went round it. All
that's changed, but thanks
to the tireless efforts of
fundraisers, artisans and
restorers, and the non-
Victoria-like generosity of
the present royals, the
building itself is a joy for
present and later
generations, and its future,
at last, is assured.

Black Rock appears to have been a pretty wild and windswept place in the 1920s. A good place to commune with the waves and follow the rock walks.

*Opposite:* The cliffs here are grandiose and sheer and add a rugged quality to the more genteel aspects of Brighton, such as Palace Pier, viewed from around the headland.

In 1936 the Black Rock Lido opened, transforming the area's fortunes and making it part of the whole Brighton experience. Magnus Volk's little railway delivered holidaymakers here from Palace Pier for forty years until it was closed in 1978 and subsequently demolished.

*Opposite:* The view eastwards serves to heighten the sense of man dwarfed by the elements. But taming those elements was very much part of the business of Brighton and the other towns on the Sussex coast.

Volk's little railway continues to run along the shoreline, though regrettably his much madder 'Daddy Long Legs' is long gone. This ran along rails often submerged by the sea, was electric powered, and consisted of a sort of Victorian conservatory, complete with aspidistras, raised above the waves on the legs from which it gained its popular name. Volk was a prime example of the sort of maverick genius Brighton nurtured, and if not all of his inventions were useful, all added quality and excitement to the life of the town.

The beach at Kemptown in the 1920s. A place with a rather bohemian air, Kemptown has always attracted artists and original thinkers. Brighton native Aubrey Beardsley made his home here, as did Lewis Carroll.

Like much of Kemptown, Hove owes its stately grandeur to the vision of father and son architects Amon and Amon Henry Wilds and their regular collaborator Charles Busby. They created Brunswick Terrace, seen here in the 1950s, between 1824 and 1830.

Between the terrace and the sea, the sweeping Brunswick Lawns epitomise the sense of space and gentility that the designers of Hove set out to achieve.

The buildings in this picture are two of the four that were once collectively known as The Lawns. That on the right is the wonderful Sackville Hotel, which once sported golden copper domes. Unmistakable for its apple green colour, towers and huge balconies, the hotel has suffered badly from the ravages of time. It was renovated in the 1960s, but suffered a serious fire in the 1990s and various collapses and disintegrations.

*Opposite, top:* Here's a shot of the other substantial edifices that made up The Lawns.

*Opposite, bottom:* The good news is that the Sackville, seen here from slightly further up the road, will not die. £5m is being spent to bring it back up to full five-star status.

Across the road from the Sackville lie Hove's exquisite bowling greens with, in the background, that other vital feature of any English seaside resort from Victorian times, the bandstand . . .

. . . or 'band enclosure', as it is described on this card, making it sound more like a precaution than a platform for musical entertainment.

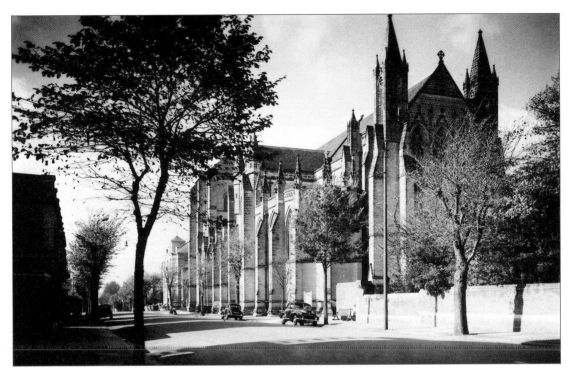

Hove's parish church of All Saints is a vast Victorian edifice, bearing a strong resemblance to Truro Cathedral. It would seem there was a very persuasive Morris Minor dealer at work in Brighton and Hove in the early 1950s.

Hove Lagoon was another masterly achievement of the planners. Opened in 1930, its layout remains much the same today, and it now provides an ideal venue for windsurfing and other watersports.

Hove wasn't all dignified terraces and manicured lawns. There was fun to be had too, as here, at sunset on the sands.

A Rover, a Standard and a couple of Fords line up neatly on the edge of the road where Hove begins and Brighton ends, *c.* 1950.

Standing some 30ft high, and marking the divide between Brighton and Hove, the Peace statue commemorates Edward VII – The Peacemaker – who came to Brighton at various times to convalesce after illness. It was designed by Newbury Trent and was unveiled to the public in October 1912.

# 2

# The Surrounding Area

Portslade Harbour in the 1930s. As sail gave way to steam Shoreham's shipbuilding days also ended, but it continues in importance as a fishing harbour.

The wooden bridge at Shoreham had recently been rebuilt when this picture was taken. The original had been constructed in 1781, so was more than ready for renewal in 1916. The new bridge closely followed the design of its eighteenth-century predecessor, yet actually formed part of the main A27 until 1971!

Here's the view towards New Shoreham after the bypass had been opened and peace returned. I wonder if he could get Southern ITV on that aerial?

The first Norfolk Bridge, seen here, was opened in 1833. It was based on the design of the famous chain bridge that links Buda and Pest across the Danube.

The Norfolk suspension bridge was replaced by this steel girder affair in 1922. A mere fifty-five years later, that too was replaced by the present concrete construction.

Although this postcard is entitled 'New Shoreham Church', we can say with some certainty that the photograph was not taken in the year 1100. It is actually referring to the ancient church at New Shoreham. The church's apparent dedication to Mary de Haura is unique, but all becomes clear when you realise that 'de Haura' refers to the church, rather than Mary. It is the church of Mary at the harbour – cf le Havre, and various other derivations of 'haven'.

When it was originally built by the Normans St Mary's was vast – over 200ft in length – but the nave collapsed in the seventeenth century, leaving it about half the intended size.

At the start of the book we saw fishing boats from Shoreham on the beach at Brighton. Here's an early photo of an open boat in its home harbour.

The sheds and stores of the fishermen in the foreground, and the two halves of Shoreham with its connecting bridge as a backdrop.

Built in 1954 and demolished in 1988, the old power station at Shoreham was a monumental feature of the local landscape. When it was built its chimneys were the tallest structures in Sussex at over 350ft.

Shoreham lighthouse was built in 1846. How long it has had that toilet block at its foot is unclear. Eighty years or more, it would appear from this picture.

West Blatchington windmill is unique in a number of ways, not least because it was painted by John Constable. Similar in principle to smock mills all over the country, it is unusual in having six rather than eight sides, and even more so in being mounted on a plinth, or tower, which raises it above the farm buildings in these pictures.

Here you can see how the base of the mill is actually higher than the roof of the adjoining barn. A 1930s road scheme marooned it on an island not long after these pictures were taken, and the long south barn, seen here and painted by Constable, was destroyed by fire in 1937.

Chattri is the word for umbrella in Urdu, Hindi and Punjabi. The monument by that name commemorates those Sikhs and Hindus who died as a result of injuries suffered on the Western Front in the First World War, and marks the spot where their bodies were cremated in accordance with their traditions.

*Opposite:* The last windmill to be built in Sussex, Patcham Mill was finished in 1885, and continued to serve the same family (Harris) until it closed in 1924. It has since been adapted into a dwelling, though its machinery is still intact.

*Opposite and above:* Long a popular spot with walkers and visitors, the Devil's Dyke is the largest chalkland dry coombe in Britain. In Victorian times a railway and even a cable car were laid on to aid punters in the appreciation of the spectacle. By the time these cards were produced in the interwar years, it had regained its natural character. Prominent devil's disciple Aleister Crowley's ashes were scattered here. Now in the hands of the National Trust and designated an Environmentally Sensitive Area, it seems set to stay that way, although not all creature comforts are excluded. The historic Devil's Dyke pub is close at hand. A major restoration project at the dyke commenced in 2002.

Holy Trinity Church at Poynings remains much as it was when built in the fourteenth century. In the background are the Dyke Hills, and the village nestles below the venerable church. Like Fulking and Edburton, it owes its existence to one of three springs emanating from the vicinity of Devil's Dyke.

A paradise for walkers, Wolstonbury Hill is part of the spectacular sweep of downland that protects Brighton from the landward side. Evidence of early settlement abounds here in the form of ancient forts, pits and burial mounds.

*Above:* The first recorded windmill at Clayton was a post mill called Duncton, erected in 1765. This was joined, in 1852, by a second mill called Lashmar, which was removed here from Brighton. In 1864 Duncton was dismantled and replaced by the brick-built tower mill seen on the right above. The two mills were christened Jack (right) and Jill (left) by visitors in the 1920s.

Sometimes called the Ditchling Mill, Oldland Mill is actually situated in Keymer, only two miles from the Jack and Jill Mills, the latter of which it resembles. Indeed, it was installed by the Medhurst family, who were responsible for both, and is today believed to be the only post mill in southern England with a steam engine to enable milling on windless days.

Also known as Wing's Place, Anne of Cleves' House in Ditchling is bound to be an attraction for a passing photographer. One of the best brick-and-timber sixteenth-century houses in Sussex, it was purportedly given to Anne by Henry VIII as a sort of settlement, when his fancy took him elsewhere.

In fact, although Henry did settle the odd property or two, including one in Lewes, it is more likely that this old manor house belonged to the aforementioned Wing.

For all that, it is the Mistress of Cleves who brings 'em in, and has continued so to do for many a long year. Whichever way you look at it, the place is a fine survival, so it has a lot to thank the old queen for.

A rare interior shot demonstrates its uniqueness and the value placed, even in the 1930s, on this jewel of history and architecture.

Ditchling High Street, with the Downs in the distance and Lloyds Bank in the foreground. No ATMs then, or call centres. All the accounts were managed in the bank chambers directly above the counter area. Of course, no more than a tenth of Ditchling's residents set foot in it or any other financial institution. The wisdom of the ancients.

*Opposite, top:* The owner of a Triumph Herald estate drops in for a quick one at the Sandrock Inn in Ditchling High Street in the late 1960s. No covering up of number plates on published photos in those days, so I hope he or she had a good reason to be there.

*Opposite, bottom:* Here's another view of Ditchling High Street, with one of the other two pubs, the Bull Hotel, in evidence. First licensed in 1636, it actually takes its name from a Papal Bull, or edict.

St Margaret's at Ditchling is very ancient. It is a cruciform church, built on a sandstone rise, and dates back to pre-Conquest times. The picture opposite is from the 1930s.

In the late twentieth century it was neater and a proper path had been provided, but not much other change had taken place sixty years on, and over a thousand years since the building of the church!

This is a view of Ditchling Beacon or the 'Black Cap', the highest point on the escarpment, now in the hands of the National Trust. It is believed that that old villain Simon de Montfort passed this way in 1264, before the Battle of Lewes. I don't think the National Trust would let him become a member.

St Lawrence's church, Falmer, in the 1920s. This scene is very little changed today, as long as you close your ears to the traffic noise. At the heart of the protracted wranglings about Brighton's need for a new sports stadium, the village becomes ever more like an exquisite period stage set in the midst of twenty-first-century mayhem.

Falmer's idyllic nature was recognised and valued eighty-odd years ago, as these artistic studies attest. Will its time warp fail at last, and the village be swamped by a combination of university campus and sporting types, to become some sassenach Brigadoon? I fear we would do well to make the most of it.

Here's the pump that served Falmer's residents for much of its history until a rather more welcome form of progress brought running water to each house.

Here are Falmer's cosy and unassuming little cottages, slumbering peacefully, with no thought of the brash outside world that would one day encircle it.

The church of St Lawrence at Telscombe dates back to 966, though there is evidence that the settlement existed in Roman times. In the eighteenth and nineteenth centuries the manor was held by the Shelley family, but the new 'lordship' who arrived in 1900 was to leave his own indelible mark upon the village.

Bookmaker Ambrose Gorham had clear ideas about what Telscombe needed and what it didn't need. And he put his money where his mouth was. When his horse, Shannon Lass, won the Grand National he spent his winnings on bringing a water supply and electric light to the village. He also carried out restorations to the church, whose guardians evidently forced themselves to accept the proceeds of gambling.

Gorham intended that the place should be a haven away from the noise that was increasing all around, so stipulated in his will that Telscombe should never have a shop or a pub. He also required that his successors as lords of the manor be smokers and drinkers! Eccentric as his methods might have been, Gorham clearly succeeded in his main endeavour to keep Telscombe from being spoiled. Little has changed from these romantic images taken a lifetime ago, and the village is now designated a conservation area. I don't know how diligently Gorham's successor, 'Squire' Smith, followed his will in the matter of tobacco and alcohol, but before his own death he gave the manor house to the National Trust.

*Opposite, top:* With only a black and white palette to work from, the photographer was hard put to it to find anything very picturesque about Peacehaven in the 1960s. It winds up here looking more like Alice Springs.

*Opposite, bottom:* And this picture doesn't help. No doubt the campers were resolutely happy, but things look a little bleak from this distance.

At least the parish church of the Ascension looks smart and new, having been consecrated in 1955.

This is Saltdean Bay before Charles Neville transformed it out of all recognition. The only house visible is the coastguard cottage and there is an open beach directly below the cliff. Already in place are the singular columns acquired from the 1924 Empire Exhibition.

Here's more or less the same view ten years later, following the completion of the undercliff in 1935. The coastguard cottage is still there, but now surrounded by buildings laid out to follow the natural contours of the land.

A closer view of the curious pillars with which Neville lined his promenade.

The striking sign that welcomed visitors to Saltdean in the 1960s.

Jump forward nearly twenty years and this photograph describes itself as 'Saltdean showing Butlin's Hotel'. The white building dominating the scene is of course the magnificent Ocean Hotel, which had originally opened in 1938. Hitler saw to it that the demand for such luxury didn't last long and it had seen out most of the war as a fire service college before being put up for sale in 1947. Six years later holiday camp magnate Billy Butlin bought 'the bargain of his life' for a quarter of a million. Hence the commemorative postcards.

Here's the distinctive drive in 1953 with Butlin's logo replacing the original Ocean Hotel sign over the entrance.

Still in Butlin's hands in the 1960s, and decorated with some of those interesting plastic lights that proliferated in seaside resorts during that not always so stylish decade.

The Ocean in the 1980s, looking prosperous, with a stylish art deco logo over the entrance. Forty years on the clientele had changed, but it was still doing it for them.

*Right and below:* Its glory days gone for ever, the future of the Ocean hung in the balance for some time. I photographed it here at its lowest ebb in 2006, awaiting conversion to 300-odd flats. At least some trace of the old place will remain, though the salons, the stairways and the bars will give way to a modern development behind the original façade, which will be retained because it alone is listed. *(Author)*

The history of Saltdean Lido is a happier one. Designed by Neville, it could accommodate 500 bathers a day, and opened in 1938. This night photograph shows the shiny new Lido with the equally new Ocean Hotel in the background.

Nearly thirty years on here's the Lido in the swimming swinging sixties, with the Butlin's Ocean Hotel occupying most of the hillside behind.

I don't know what that dog hopes to gain by hanging about outside Mr Hilder's butcher's shop. This image paints a tranquil picture of Rottingdean that wasn't always accurate. The Kiplings and the Burne-Joneses were not at all versed in the behaviour expected of the gentry in these parts. When one of them suggested Britain had been wrong in one of its military enterprises all hell broke loose.

This is Sir Edward Burne-Jones's house, North End House, and a finer property for an artist is hard to imagine. Largely self-taught, Burne-Jones was a leading light of the Pre-Raphaelites. His stained glass adorns the church at Rottingdean, and there is a moving museum to him in the village.

The successful Burne-Jones had three very different houses combined into one. By the time of this photograph in about 1972, they had gone their separate but connected ways.

The so-called 'Tudor Close' in Rottingdean was actually completed in 1929 by that same Charles Neville responsible for Peacehaven. It was created out of the barns and cowsheds of Court Farm and run as a luxury hotel. Neville claimed it was better known in Hollywood than in England, and it certainly numbered the likes of Bette Davis and Cary Grant as long-term guests.

Described on the card as 'The Granary', these houses at the entrance to Dean Court Road were originally farm buildings belonging to Court Farm. They were converted into mock-Tudor dwellings at about the time of this photograph in the 1930s.

Not much has changed in this view from the opposite direction – towards the windmill – in the early 1970s.

St Margaret's church at Rottingdean. The elaborate lych gate was added in 1897, though the church itself dates back to before 1100.

The tower on the Norman church fell down causing a great deal of damage after a 'mere' hundred years or so, so the church was rebuilt in Early English style, with walls of a prodigious thickness, and has stood the test of time since.

The dreaded double-yellow lines had made their appearance in Rottingdean by the 1970s. The Olde Place and the Dene Hotel face each other across the bright new official boundary here.

'Rottingdean, Old Cottages' proclaims the title of this postcard, but they are again those cottages that were new when the photo was taken – the renovated, Tudorised buildings of Dean Court Road.

The old Norton House Hotel had ceased to be such before this picture was taken in the 1950s.

The Elms, Kipling's house at Rottingdean before he moved his family to the more extensive accommodations at Bateman's near Burmarsh. A large part of the gardens here, which started out as common land, have now been bought back and made available for public enjoyment.

The lone horseman on page 119 has given way to the Hillman Minx, the Mini and the Vauxhall Victor estate in this view of The Elms in the 1970s.

Rottingdean windmill was moved to its present site in 1802. Although not always identified, it is famous far and wide as the symbol for Heinemann, the publishers.

'The valley of Rota's people', with the Downs beyond. Although the village has carried the name of a Saxon chief in one form or another for the last 1,500 years – Rotingeden, Ruttingedene, Rottyngden, Rottendeane and so forth – there's plenty of evidence of habitation here long before he, or his people, came crashing through the trees. Burial mounds on Beacon Hill date back more than 3,000 years.

This is a bit of a funny picture. Entitled 'The Downs near Rottingdean', it features a skeletal contraption half-embedded in a collapsed haystack, with a small settlement some way in the distance. The contraption might be some kind of Heath-Robinson threshing machine, but it looks for all the world like the remains of an abandoned motor. Either way, it seems a strange subject for a postcard.

Not a little of the Sussex coast has been claimed by the sea over the centuries. Even in the recent past whole houses, hotels and villages have disappeared from eroded cliff tops. The ferocity and persistence of the waves and the effectiveness of man's defences are both dramatically evidenced in these pictures of the coast at Rottingdean.

Work began on the defences in 1921. Groynes were constructed along with a flint-faced concrete sea wall. The cliff face itself was cut back to an angle of 72° to minimise the impact of weathering.

Because the work was accomplished with little more than picks, shovels and manpower, it was not completed until 1935. These pictures were taken to celebrate the scheme's success. With few modifications it has remained the model for the battle against erosion elsewhere along the coast.

A couple of ducks contemplate the meaning of life at the edge of Rottingdean's village pond with St Margaret's in the background.

The ancient village of Ovingdean is now incorporated into the City of Brighton & Hove. Founded in Saxon times by one Ofa, it seems to have led a fairly tranquil existence ever since. It is now designated a conservation area and retains much of the charm exhibited in these photographs from the 1920s.

There has been some improvement to the roads, of course, with an inevitable change of emphasis, as this has made it easier to get there.

There were only ever three churches in England dedicated to St Wulfran. Both of the others were in Lincolnshire, one at Grantham, the other at Dorrington. The latter has since ceased to be. Ovingdean's was built in the eleventh century.

The Grange was the subject of a novel, *Ovingdean Grange: A Tale of the South Downs* by Harrison Ainsworth, in which Charles II stayed overnight there and fathered a child before disappearing to France. In fact, he stayed at the George in Brighton, or was it the King's Head?

The extraordinary Undercliff Walk at Ovingdean was designed by then Borough Engineer David Edwards. It was begun in 1928, and this card celebrates its opening in 1933.

Initially founded by the sisters Penelope, Millicent and Dorothy Lawrence in 1885, Roedean moved to its dramatically impressive premises set in 40 acres of the Downs in 1898. The school's reputation went before it in the sense that it now gets the kind of results the general public assumed it always did, but a Roedean education never held any girl back.

As evening descends over the peaceful fishing town of Brighton in the early years of the twentieth century, no one is dreaming that 100 years on it will be one of the most vibrant cities in all England.

The last rays of sunset mark an appropriate ending for this photographic excursion into Brighton's past.

# JUDGES POSTCARDS
## *A brief history*

*There is every chance that the postcard you send home from your holiday started life in Sussex. Since 1904 Hastings has been the home of Judges, one of Britain's leading publishers of quality picture postcards.*

When Fred Judge arrived in Hastings in 1902 he could have had little idea of the worldwide impact he was to make on the business of postcard publishing. But he was a master with a camera and a natural entrepreneur. Fred Judge was born in Yorkshire in 1872. Photography was always his real interest, and it was while visiting Sussex in 1902 that he made the decision to give up engineering for a career as a photographer.

Fred and his brother Thomas purchased an existing business in Hastings and set up as photographers and photographic dealers under the name of Judges Photo Stores. Although the idea of sending an illustrated card through the post was not new (the first having appeared towards the end of the nineteenth century) Fred made his mark by setting himself extremely high artistic standards. At first he concentrated on local scenes and activities. Having taken his pictures he would go straight back to the darkroom to make them into postcards; these were often ready for sale within a few hours, and the quality of his work was such that passers-by would gather outside the shop window for a sight of his latest offering.

Technically stunning, and using all the latest photographic technology, Freds pictures won over 100 medals, and one-man exhibitions of his work were held in London, Washington, New York and Tokyo.

Back in Hastings the business was expanding, necessitating moves to bigger and better premises, culminating in the move in 1927 to the purpose-built factory that the company occupies to this day. Although the building has been developed and extended, the Italianate façade remains a famous landmark on the A259 coast road.

Fred Judge died in February 1950 at the age of 78, having built up an internationally respected company. The business was sold to another Judges photographer, who introduced lithographic colour printing. Then in 1984 Judges became a real family concern once again when Bernard and Jan Wolford took over. It became even more of a family business when their son Graeme, now managing director, joined, followed by Trevor, now sales director. The present management can truly be said to be building on the foundations laid by Fred Judge over ninety years ago.

*Judges Postcards Ltd, 176 Bexhill Road, St Leonards on Sea,*
*East Sussex, TN38 8BN*
*Tel: 01424 420919; Fax: 01424 438538*